Ruthless Rhymes

Verses by
Harry Graham

Illustrations by

and Ridgewell

Edward Arnold

© V. Thesiger 1984

First published in Great Britain 1984 by
Edward Arnold (Publishers) Ltd,
41 Bedford Square, London WC1B 3DQ

Edward Arnold (Australia) Pty Ltd,
80 Waverley Road, Caulfield East,
Victoria 3145, Australia

Edward Arnold, 300 North Charles Street,
Baltimore, Maryland 21201, USA

This edition is a combination of Harry Graham's
Ruthless Rhymes for Heartless Homes, illustrated
by GH (1900; Graham used the pseudonym
'Col. D. Streamer'), and his *More Ruthless Rhymes
for Heartless Homes*, illustrated by Ridgewell
(1930). *Most Ruthless Rhymes* combined the two
in 1974, but omitted some of the verses and their
accompanying illustrations; the present edition
is the first unabridged combination.

British Library Cataloguing in Publication Data

Graham, Harry, *1874–1936*
    Ruthless rhymes.
    I. Title   II. Ridgewell
    821'.8   PR6013.R18

    ISBN 0-7131-6426-3

Display type Gilleon set by Face.

Text set in 12/13 pt Garamond Compugraphic
by Colset Pte Ltd, Singapore.
Printed in Great Britain by
Richard Clay (The Chaucer Press) Ltd,
Bungay, Suffolk

Dedication to E.P.G.

With the most profound respect,
I inscribe my dedication,
Realising its effect
On this volume's circulation;
Since your name can hardly fail
To command a ready sale.

If the sunshine of your smile
Lights our work, nor wanders off it,
Self and artist, in a while,
Hope to share a handsome profit;
But, if you (and Fate) are cross,
Mr Arnold bears the loss.

Do, I beg you, realise
Your responsible position,
If this book should ever rise
To a third or fourth edition;
Understand what you have done
If it fails to weather one!

Contents

Author's Preface

With guilty, conscience-stricken tears
   I offer up these rhymes of mine
To children of maturer years
   (From seventeen to ninety-nine).
A special solace may they be
In days of second infancy.

The frenzied mother who observes
   This volume in her offspring's hand,
And trembles for the darling's nerves,
   Must very clearly understand,
If Baby suffers, by and by,
The ARTIST is to blame, not I.

But should the little brat survive,
   And fatten on the Ruthless Rhyme,
To found a Heartless Home, and thrive
   Through a successful life of crime,
The Artist hopes that you will see
That *I* am to be thanked, not *he*.

Fond parent, you whose children are
   Of tender age (from two to eight),
Pray keep this little volume far
   .From Baby's reach, and relegate
My Verses to an upper shelf,
Where you may study them yourself!

The Stern Parent

Father heard his Children scream,
So he threw them in the stream,
Saying as he drowned the third,
"Children should be seen, *not* heard!"

Indifference

When Grandmamma fell off the boat,
And couldn't swim (and wouldn't float),
Matilda just stood by and smiled.
I almost could have slapped the child.

Nurse's Mistake

Nurse, who peppered baby's face
(She mistook it for a muffin),
Held her tongue and kept her place,
"Layin' low and sayin' nuffin' ";
Mother, seeing baby blinded,
Said, "Oh, nurse, how absent-minded!"

Providence

Fate moves in a mysterious way,
As shown by Uncle Titus,
Who unexpectedly, one day,
Was stricken with St Vitus.
It proved a blessing in disguise,
For, thanks to his condition,
He won the Non-Stop Dancing Prize
At Wembley Exhibition.

Jim; or,
the Deferred
Luncheon Party

When the line he tried to cross,
The express ran into Jim;
Bitterly I mourn his loss—
I was to have lunched with him.

Consolation

I sliced a brassey-shot at Rye,
And killed a luckless passer-by.
The ball rebounded off his head
And, landing on the green, lay dead.
His widow it must much console
To know 'twas thus I won the hole.

The Fond Father

Of Baby I was very fond,
She'd won her father's heart;
So, when she fell into the pond,
It gave me quite a start.

Tragedy

That morning, when my wife eloped
With James, our chauffeur, how
   I moped!
What tragedies in life there are!
I'm dashed if I can start the car!

Equanimity

Aunt Jane observed, the second time
She tumbled off a bus,
"The step is short from the Sublime
To the Ridiculous."

Presence
of Mind

When, with my little daughter Blanche,
I climbed the Alps, last summer,
I saw a dreadful avalanche
About to overcome her;
And, as it swept her down the slope,
I vaguely wondered whether
I should be wise to cut the rope
That held us twain together.

I must confess I'm glad I did,
But still I miss the child—poor kid!

Tender-Heartedness

Billy, in one of his nice new sashes,
Fell in the fire and was burnt to ashes;
Now, although the room grows chilly,
I haven't the heart to poke poor Billy.

Compensation

Weep not for little Léonie,
Abducted by a French *Marquis*!
Though loss of honour was a wrench,
Just think how it's improved her French!

Unselfishness

All those who see my children say,
"What sweet, what kind, what charming
    elves!"
They are so thoughtful, too, for they
Are *always* thinking of themselves,
It must be ages since I ceased
To wonder which I liked the least.

Such is their generosity,
That, when the roof began to fall,
They would not share the risk with me,
But said, "No, father, take it all!"
Yet I should love them more, I know,
If I did not dislike them so.

Discipline

To Percival, my youngest son,
Who cut his sister's throat for fun,
I said: "Now, Percy! Manners, please!
You really mustn't be a tease!
I shall refuse, another time,
To take you to the Pantomime!"

The Englishman's Home

I was playing golf the day
That the Germans landed;
All our troops had run away,
All our ships were stranded;
And the thought of England's shame
Altogether spoilt my game.

Obstinacy

I warned poor Mary of her fate,
But she *would* wed a plumber's mate!
For hours the choir was forced to sing
While he went back to fetch the ring.

Appreciation

Auntie, did you feel no pain
Falling from that willow tree?
Will you do it, please, again?
'Cos my friend here didn't see.

Uplift

It seems that with Eternal Youth
Great-Grandmamma is gifted,
For though (to tell the honest truth)
Her face has twice been "lifted",
Today she doesn't look to me
A minute more than ninety-three.

Obstruction

You know "Lord's"? Well, once I
   played there,
And a ball I hit to leg
Struck the umpire's head and
   stayed there,
As a nest retains an egg.

Hastily the wicket-keeper
Seized a stump and prized about.

Had it gone two inches deeper
He would ne'er have run me out.

This I minded all the more,
As my stroke was well worth four.

Carelessness

A window-cleaner in our street
Who fell (five storeys) at my feet
Impaled himself on my umbrella.
I said: "Come, come, you careless fella!
If my umbrella had been shut
You might have landed on my nut!"

Self-Sacrifice

Father, chancing to chastise
His indignant daughter, Sue,
Said, "I hope you realise
That this hurts me more than you."

Susan straight ceased to roar;
"If that's really true," said she,
"I can stand a good deal more;
Pray go on, and don't mind me."

L'Enfant Glacé

When Baby's cries grew hard to bear
I popped him in the Frigidaire.
I never would have done so if
I'd known that he'd be frozen stiff.
My wife said: "George, I'm so
    unhappé!
Our darling's now completely *frappé*!"

The Shark

Bob was bathing in the bay,
When a Shark who passed that way
Punctured him in seven places
—And he made *such* funny faces!

Winter Sports

The ice upon our pond's so thin
That poor Mamma has fallen in!
We cannot reach her from the shore
Until the surface freezes more.
Ah me, my heart grows weary waiting—
Besides, I want to have some skating.

Careless Jane

Jane, who shot her Uncle Bill,
Said his death did not affect her,
But, which makes it sadder still,
Broke my "Hammerless Ejector".

Thoughtlessness

I never shall forget my shame
To find my son had forged my name.
If he'd had any thought for others
He might at least have forged his
    mother's.

Impetuous
Samuel

Sam had spirits nought could check,
And today, at breakfast, he
Broke his baby-sister's neck,
So he shan't have jam for tea!

Opportunity

When Mrs Gorm (Aunt Eloïse)
Was stung to death by savage bees,
Her husband (Prebendary Gorm)
Put on his veil, and took the swarm.
He's publishing a book, next May,
On "How to Make Bee-keeping Pay".

Calculating
Clara

O'er the rugged mountain's brow
Clara threw the twins she nursed,
And remarked, "I wonder now
Which will reach the bottom first?"

Lord Gorbals

Once, as old Lord Gorbals motored
Round his moors near John o' Groats,
He collided with a goatherd
And a herd of forty goats.
By the time his car got through
They were all defunct but two.

Roughly he addressed the goatherd:
"Dash my whiskers and my corns!
Can't you teach your goats, you dotard,
That they ought to sound their horns?
Look, my AA badge is bent!
I've a mind to raise your rent!"

London Calling

When rabies attacked my Uncle Daniel,
And he had fits of barking like a spaniel,
The BBC relayed him (from all stations)
At *Children's Hour* in "farmyard
  imitations".

Inconsiderate Hannah

Naughty little Hannah said
She could make her Grandma whistle,
So, that night, inside her bed,
Placed some nettles and a thistle.

Though dear Grandma quite infirm is,
Heartless Hannah watched her settle,
With her poor old epidermis
Resting up against a nettle.

Suddenly she reached the thistle!
My! you should have heard her whistle.

A successful plan was Hannah's,
But I cannot praise her manners.

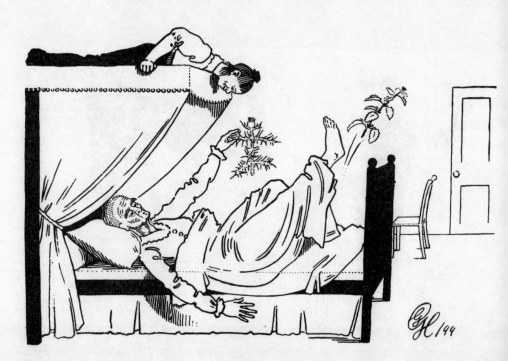

Quiet Fun

My son Augustus, in the street, one day,
Was feeling quite exceptionally merry.
A stranger asked him: "Can you show
   me pray,
The quickest way to Brompton
   Cemetery?"
"The quickest way? You bet I can!"
   said Gus,
And pushed the fellow underneath a bus.

Whatever people say about my son,
He does enjoy his little bit of fun.

Philip

Philip, foozling with his cleek,
Drove his ball through Helen's cheek;

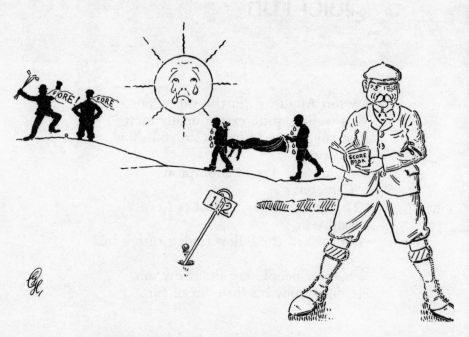

Sad they bore her corpse away,
"Seven up and six to play."

Thrift

Last week our Parlourmaid withdrew
Her savings from the Bank,
And sailed away to far Peru.
Next day, her vessel sank!
She perished in an upper bunk,
And thus her sinking-fund was sunk.

Misfortunes Never Come Singly

Making toast at the fireside,
Nurse fell in the grate and died;

And, what makes it ten times worse,
All the toast was burnt *with* nurse.

The Last Straw

Oh, gloomy, gloomy was the day
When poor Aunt Bertha ran away!
But Uncle finds today more black:
Aunt Bertha's threatening to run back!

The Perils of Obesity

Yesterday my gun exploded
When I thought it wasn't loaded;
Near my wife I pressed the trigger,
Chipped a fragment off her figure.

'Course I'm sorry, and all that,
But she shouldn't be so fat.

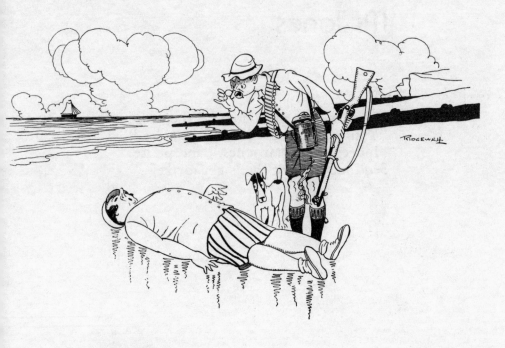

Bull's-Eye

At rifle-practice on the sands at Deal,
I fired at what I took to be a seal.
When later on I learnt 'twas sister Florrie
And that I'd shot her, I was very sorry.
But still it gratified me just a trifle
To find myself so expert with a rifle,
For, with so large a target as my sister,
I should have been a duffer if I'd
     missed her.

Mr Jones

"There's been an accident!" they said,
"Your servant's cut in half; he's dead!"
"Indeed!" said Mr Jones, "and please
Send me the half that's got my keys."

Grandpapa

Grandpapa fell down a drain;
Couldn't scramble out again.
Now he's floating down the sewer
There's one grandpapa the fewer.

La Course Interrompue I

Jean, qui allait à Dijon
(Il montait en bicyclette),
Rencontra un gros lion
Qui se faisait la toilette.

La Course Interrompue II

Voila Jean qui tompe à terre,
Et le lion le digère!

Mon Dieu! Que c'est embêtant
Il me devait quatre francs.

Waste

Our governess—would you believe
It?—drowned herself on Christmas Eve!
This was a waste, as, any way,
It would have been a holiday.

Aunt

Aunt, a most delightful soul
But with little self-control,
When run over by a "taxi",
Grew unconscionably waxy.

She could not have made more fuss
Had it been a motor-bus!

Bishop Prout

In Burma, once, while Bishop Prout
Was preaching on Predestination,
There came a sudden waterspout
And drowned the congregation.
"O Heav'n!" cried he, "why can't
  you wait
Until they've handed round the plate!"

Uncle

Uncle, whose inventive brains
Kept evolving aeroplanes,
Fell from an enormous height
On my garden lawn, last night.
Flying is a fatal sport,
Uncle wrecked the tennis-court.

Canon Gloy

One morning, just as Canon Gloy
Was starting gaily for the station,
The Doctor said: "Your eldest boy
Must have another operation!"
"What!" cried the Canon. "Not again?
That's *twice* he's made me miss
    my train!"

Necessity

Late last night I slew my wife,
Stretched her on the parquet flooring;
I was loth to take her life,
But I *had* to stop her snoring!

Patience

When skiing in the Engadine
My hat blew off down a ravine.
My son, who went to fetch it back,
Slipped through an icy glacier's crack
And then got permanently stuck.
It really was infernal luck:
My hat was practically new—
I loved my little Henry too—
And I may have to wait for years
Till either of them reappears.

Aunt Eliza

In the drinking-well
Which the plumber built her,
Aunt Eliza fell . . . .

. . . . We must buy a filter.

Black and Tan

Sun-bathing on the beach at Dover,
My wife became dark brown all over.
Upon the esplanade a man
Mistook her for the Aga Khan.
Another asked her—still more cruel—
To sing a Negro Spiritual.
While on the Pier (where jokes are cheap)
They called her "The Calcutta Sweep".

Inconvenience

I collided with some "trippers"
In my swift De Dion Bouton;
Squashed them out as flat as kippers,
Left them "aussi mort que mouton".
What a nuisance "trippers" are!
I must now repaint the car.

Mother

When a child of tender age,
I'd a monkey in a cage.
Now I have no need for pets,
Mother's joined the Suffragettes.

Darling

Baby in the cauldron fell,
See the grief on Mother's brow
Mother loved her darling well,
Darling's quite hardboiled by now!

Uncle Joe

Poor Uncle Joe has gone, you know,
To rest beyond the stars.
I miss him, oh! I miss him so!
(He had *such* good cigars.)

Father
During dinner at the Ritz,
Father kept on having fits,
And, which made my sorrow greater,
I was left to tip the waiter.

Waste
I had written to Aunt Maud,
Who was on a trip abroad,
When I heard she'd died of cramp,
Just too late to save the stamp.

Baby
Baby roused its father's ire,
By a cold and formal lisp,
So he placed it on the fire,
And reduced it to a crisp.
Mother said, "Oh, stop a bit!
This is *over*doing it!"

Mabel
Mabel's chronic inflammation
Led at length to amputation.
Oh, her cries were loud and deep!
I could scarcely get to sleep.

The Children's Don't I

Don't tell Papa his nose is red
As any rosebud or geranium;
Forbear to eye his hairless head
Or criticise his cootlike cranium;
'Tis years of sorrow and of care
Have made his head come through
  his hair.

The Children's Don't II

Don't give your endless guinea-pig
(Wherein that animal may build a
Sufficient nest) the Sunday wig
Of poor, dear, dull, deaf Aunt Matilda.
Oh, *don't* tie string across her path,
Or empty beetles in her bath!

The Children's Don't III

Don't ask your Uncle why he's fat;
Avoid upon his toe-joints treading;
Don't hide a hedgehog in his hat,
Or bury brushes in his bedding.
He will not see the slightest sport
In pepper put into his port!

The Children's Don't IV

Don't pull away the cherished chair
On which Mamma intended sitting,
Nor yet prepare her session there
By setting on the seat her knitting;
Pause ere you hurt her spine, I pray—
That is a game that *two* can play.

Scorching John

John, who rode his Dunlop tyre
O'er the head of sweet Maria,

When she died in frightful pain,
Had to blow it out again.